The Marksman

Books by Jeff Friedman

The Record-Breaking Heat Wave
Scattering the Ashes
Taking Down the Angel
Black Threads
Working in Flour
Pretenders
Floating Tales
The Marksman

Translations
Memorials: A Selection by Mieczslaw Jastrun with Dzvinia Orlowsky
Two Gardens: Modern Hebrew Poems of the Bible with Nati Zohar

The Marksman

by Jeff Friedman

Carnegie Mellon University Press
Pittsburgh 2020

Acknowledgments

My thanks to the editors of the following publications in which these poems first appeared:

Alive Magazine: "Legerdemain"
The American Journal of Poetry: "The Escaped Creatures Offer a Blessing"
Café Irreal: "Whistling"
The Cincinnati Review: "Dust"
December: "Burial," "The Marksman," and "Let the Old Man Go"
Hotel Amerika: "My Money" and "What My Father Heard"
KYSO Flash: "Forgiveness"
Mudlark: "Fox at the Door"
North Dakota Quarterly: "How to Make It"
Plume: "Counting Orgasms," "How to Walk on Water," "They Fire at Us,"
    "The Void," "Truth," "Counterpunch," "Risen," "Zero," "Not Much," and
    "What They Take, What They Leave"
Poetry International: "What Happened to the Country," "With My Enemy,"
    and "Be a Bigger Person"
Red Wheelbarrow: "Stories," "One Hand Clapping," and "Patriarchs"
Serving House Journal: "Old Grievance"
SurVision: "Wet Angel," "In the Promised Land," and "Man on the Flying
    Trapeze"
Sukoon: "Demagogue"

Early versions of "Old Grievance" and "Forgiveness" initially appeared in *Sukoon* in a much different form. "Let the Old Man Go" and "Ode to Yahweh" were reprinted in the anthology *Imagining the Jewish God*. My thanks to Celia Bland, Steven Schreiner, Colleen Randall, Charna Meyers, Ellen Geist, Bill Doreski, Sharon Dolin, Jennifer Militello, Ross Gay, Stephanie Smith, and Nin Andrews for their help on individual pieces. I also wish to thank Dzvinia Orlowsky, Chard deNiord, and Roy Nathanson for reading and commenting on drafts of my manuscript.

Book design by Shruti Murali

Library of Congress Control Number 2020943668
ISBN 978-0-88748-659-3

10 9 8 7 6 5 4 3 2 1

for Colleen

You can be proud of yourself, False Angel, for the faded tails
        of dying comets
for killing a man already dead,
for weeping a tireless stream of tears over a shadow
for smothering the air in its last breath.

—Rafael Alberti

Contents

3

Dust

From the weatherman comes a forecast of dust.
From the red-bearded prophets come
the desserts of the desert and the covenant
of wild asses braying out the candles on their cakes.
From the mountains come the rocks
and the layers of wisdom grinding their teeth.
And from the old dust comes the new dust
with the promise of more covenants to come.
And from the great flood come the great dryness
and the doves plunging toward the arc of light.
From the rainbow comes multicolored dust,
and from the body come seven kinds of dust,
and from the spider's web, filaments of dust
and from the memory of our mothers and fathers
comes the smell of dust, and from the smell
come more memories and the voices whispering like dust,
and the debris from their skin, swirling
in wind. And the debris clings to our lips and tongues.
From the gritty particles comes the bitter taste,
and from the crows' wings a dark dust falls,
and from the clouds a white dust hovers above us.
And dust cleans our windshield
so we can see more clearly what's ahead.

I

Demagogue

The lie spread from his lips and tongue
like a sweet syllable, and it spread
from his fingertips like rays of light

and it spread from his legs and hips like music
and it spread from his skin like a pungent odor.
And then it spread from window to window,

like a piece of blue sky, and then it walked
over the river and then it strutted through town
clicking its taps on the pavement, and then

the wind carried the news of the lie
from clothesline to clothesline, from tent to tent.
It flew from the mouths of men and women

hunching over their worktables, flew
from the lips of cats stalking squirrels,
flew from the jaws of spiders,

from their sticky legs, flew from the nests
of crows over ragged rooftops. It flew
at the sun, bursting into bright fears,

its bitter truth showering over us.

My Money

My money won't buy me a condo,
a new car or even a good dinner.
It won't shell out a dime for movies,
new clothes, or doctor bills.
My money flashes on screen
like kills in a warrior video game;
bells go off. My money is happy
where it is, doing nothing,
watching me as I watch it.
Like M.C. Hammer, my money says,
"U can't touch this," claiming it will multiply
if I never spend it. My money
is useless, but I think about it anyway,
stacks of bills in cyberspace
showering over black soil.
There's so much I could buy,
and I might even pay off some debts—
but the scanners
can't find anything in my accounts
because when I go to spend it,
my money hides from everyone,
including me. My money won't even
buy me a dollar, yet it's spreading
like a fog that gets in your eye,
that causes tears to burn your cheeks,
spreading like bits of dust
that coat your tongue
and cause you to spit and spit
and lose your taste for everything.

What Happened to the Country

Some say the president declared the country his and took
it home. Some say the country was wild turkeys waddling
under the blind blue sky, deer leaping into the foliage, but
hunters dispatched them into the next world. Some say that
even though hundreds of trucks cranked their winches, the
country sank into the quagmire and pulled the trucks down
with it, bubbles bursting on the surface. Some say you can still
find the country if you have the right map, but so many have
followed their maps, disappearing without leaving behind a
note or a sign. Though many remember the country with tears
in their eyes, and many salute when they hear it called by
name, though some decry the country as a false brotherhood,
others believe it was an idea, and ideas evolve into other ideas
or evaporate like rain beaded on window frames whose glass
has been shattered. Without a country, without a piece of land,
there is nothing to fight over, and now all of us are refugees
walking in twos or threes toward nowhere anyone can imagine.

The Marksman

I shot the points off a star
dangling in a window
and I shot the lies
off the tongue of a liar,
who then spoke sweetly
about the pleasures of the truth.
I shot a spider before it could eat
a blue fly caught in its web.
When I blew the web apart,
the blue fly said a prayer for me,
then flew off as though on a mission.
As a bald man rose in front of me,
I shot the last clump of hair
off his pate, and he thanked me
for freeing him from the tyranny of hair.
I shot out the eyes of an old shoe
who stumbled to the river
and fell in, floating for days in the reeds.
I shot the fringe from black feathers
falling from the sky.
While the clouds bulked above me,
I riddled them
with bullets until the rain fell
and then I shot fat holes
in the raindrops
until the rain became drizzle.
When the fires came,
I shot holes in the throats of flames
and I shot the smoke too,
even as it blinded me.
And the echoes swallowed my bullets
and the holes grew lonely.

Guns

They aim at us in shops
while we browse racks of clothing,
in grocery stores wheeling our carts
down the long aisles, at gas stations
while we slide our credit cards
and press the buttons. They aim
at us where we sit to eat our dinners,
where we lie down at night,
where we make love and sleep.

Blast after blast—
some of us slump over gently, afraid
to hit the ground hard.
Some fall, still holding their keys.
Some, in movie theaters, crumple
in their seats, popcorn
popping in their mouths,
and some lie on the floor of dance clubs,
breathing into their cell phones.

Some clutch their wallets or purses
as if to protect themselves from thieves.
Some drop to the ground
face first, while others
fleeing over rooftops imagine
invisible nets before they plunge
into the pavement.
Guns rattle off our misdeeds
as bullets crash through our bodies,
looking for a home.

Patriarchs

When patriarchs meet,
they hug each other
and weep and praise their gods
and the fish in their streams

and the oil in their tanks.
They take aim at deer,
hating their white tails
and the disease that breeds in their coats.

When they meet, they vow
to cleanse the skies, to bring
back the angels of their youth,
to sweep out the dust of centuries.

Patriarchs know a good deal
when they see it, earning
compound interest on investments,
lighting up universes

in cyberspace, inspiring bibles
of bigotry. They steal off
with their Abishags
to private islands, only to lose them

to younger versions of themselves,
basking in the sun like lizards.
They lie down in hate
and rise up in greed. They shoot

holes in wisdom, for wisdom
knows too much and helps no one.
They sacrifice their rams and goats
so they won't be the next to go.

They wear heavy crowns,
slumping on thrones. They walk
out on the waters, cast their nets—
gut whole generations.

Truth

Tell the truth only if you have to
because it'll blacken your eye
or break your nose or knock out a tooth.

The truth'll lead you to stumble
into a pit so deep you can't climb out,
the sun bleeding on your face,

the moon feverish and cold. The truth'll
draw lightning, and lightning will split the tree
and the trunk will crush a thousand shadows.

Tell the truth only if you are forced to utter
the somber words that will bring down your house
and cause your family to flee from you, and

your friends to come after you with clubs and knives,
and bridges will buckle under the weight of those words,
and roads will collapse. The truth is salt, ground

into your wound, fire burning the oils
of your hands—raised against each other.
It's earth closing around you, air choking on air.

Better not to speak. Better to keep the truth
in your belly and let out only lies and foul air,
while bugs fly in your spit.

Sacrifice

You didn't lie on a makeshift altar
or plead with your father to go home,
nor did you ask about the ram,
and your father didn't lift his knife high into the sun

as if hoping it would fly from his hand
and lodge in the belly of a cloud,
and the angel never appeared
because God never sent an angel,

nor did God ask for a sacrifice,
instead remaining silent as the rocks
or the dust whipping over the rocks.
And the knife, poised to plunge into your heart,

glinted in memory only. And no ram
bleated from the bush, and no ram
died that day instead of you. The sun
was brutal, but there was no pardon or reprieve,

and when your last breath dripped
from your lips, your father
didn't whisper his love in your ear
or kneel to kiss your cheek

Let the Old Man Go

Let the old man rant about injustice again
as the wind blows in his face
as he spits and spits to clear
the phlegm and bile from his throat.
Let him berate the belligerent
bravado of the blue jays defending
their territory against his incursions.
Let him break his covenant with the beasts,
disown his own broken promises
and those who believe in them.
Let him go down on his knees
and feign humility for the clouds
and sun. They can't hear or see him.
Let him recall his old lovers
and repeat each story as if it were new.
Let him receive his gifts with open arms.
He boasts of his bravery
and his battles for righteousness
though the words sour
in your ears. Soon bitterness
will fill his belly again
and he will storm into the windows,
storm through the veils and masks,
storm against the raw faces
behind the barricades,
and nothing will stop him
but the salt in his blood.
Let him spread his final truths
for the wind will blow his words
into broken syllables, dust and rain.
Let him fall from your hands
as ash, bits of bone, impotent seed,
a last tiny ember burning out
on your fingertip.

Crossing Over

We slouched toward the ocean
of nothing, waiting for the beast
to take us. We held
hands with air and kissed
the clouds. We danced
over broken shells with bloody feet.
We lit candles for the coming of the coming,
for Moses lost in the maze of mirrors,
the light repeating itself until eternity
began again. We chalked our names
on doors and windows.
We called out our crimes
and wind carried them across
continents of shit and piss,
and hawks shrieked
and crows prophesied a reckoning
and trucks rolled over skulls
and the crushed bones of skulls crossed
great rivers. We pleaded for mercy
even as it devoured us.

They Fire at Us

They fire at us
when we walk down Main Street.
The bullets rip into the bodies
of cars. Bones fly apart.
They fire at us
when we raise our arms

when we wave
our white flags. Crows
fall from the sky, clouds
of dark feathers hover above us.
Parking meters lose their heads.

The bullets find those
who run into alleys, those
who kneel and pray,
those who sing for peace.
The bullets mark the spot,
draw the boundaries.

They fire at us
when we tell the truth
or lie. They fire into the eyes
of shadows, into the dust
swirling around us,
into our cries for help.

The bullets tear
up our blankets, leave
holes where our dreams
no longer sleep.

Not Much

Not much left here
after the bodies have been carted out,
only some specks of glass

that escaped the vacuums,
only a few stains
that couldn't be scrubbed out.

Not much left once the bullet shells
and casings were collected,
the guns bagged,

and the cracked cellphones
with their desperate messages
piled into a box and then removed.

Not much—only the bright eyes
opening in the walls where
the bullets lodged, the silent

sky breathing in the windows,
the answers breaking
into particles, and the lingering

smell of smoke.
Not much except
a stray hornet

drawing invisible loops
in the air before it settles
briefly on the light fixture.

Other

Other came from the broken vow,
raw as an egg, from shed skin,
and desire shredded to dust.
Other came from the wound
and the paste spread on the wound.
He came from the scar and the wrinkle.
No angels flew down a ladder.
No God wrestled him,
no priest declared him godly,
no warrior called him brother,
but despite the crow gnawing
at his fingers, despite his mother
denying his birth and his father wanting
to sell him to another family,
he became Other.
Other of the salty tongue,
Other of the wounded vanity,
Other of the beast torn in two.
Other sucked in the clouds
and spit them out, hard as rocks.
Other cracked the sky
in pieces with his forehead.
But there were moments
when Other carried his bundle
of sorrows through the streets,
when women laughed at his pale fuzz
and men laughed at his tree trunk legs,
when animals growled at him
when even his own dog betrayed him.
Then he wrung the necks
of spirits, seized his own ghosts
and ate them. Then he lit a candle
for himself and blew it out.

In the Promised Land

"What has been promised?" I ask. "Nothing," the voice in the
burning bush answers. "But it is all yours." When I grip a
handful of dirt, the earth grasps my arms so tightly I drop the
dirt. "This is mine," the earth says. When I bend down to drink
from the stream, the water retreats from my lips. I cup my
hands to lift it, but the water vanishes, leaving only rocks and
dried bed. I throw a rock to see if it'll find the water, but the
rock bounces until the dirt catches it. I pluck the fruit of a tree
and bite into it. The fruit tastes so bitter I spit it out. Whooping,
hyenas tear into the body of a dead animal, crushing its bones
in their jaws. Sheep bleat in the hills. A shadow flashes its dark
blade. The flame burns in a thousand burning bushes. "It's all
yours," they say to anyone foolish enough to listen.

2

How to Make It

Dance on glass shards
until your feet bleed
and the blood crusts.
Lie down on a bed of nails
and rise full of holes
and let the wind play
its melody through your body.
Sing the words and ask
everyone to sing along with you.
Steal the emptiness from your pockets
and plant it in the dirt.
Toss it into the open mouths
lying on the ground,
covered in newspapers
or wilted cornstalks.
Toss it into the crowds
as they clamor for more.
Toss it into the throats
of the wild animals who follow
you in packs. Chew it
yourself until emptiness
blossoms on your lips.
Stab the ghosts that swirl
around you, even though
the ghosts will never bleed
or stop swirling around you.
Take off your skin
and shimmy your skeleton,
waiting for applause or laughter.
Rub your bones together
until they burn.

Luck

For luck, I threw handfuls
of salt over my shoulder
but the salt burned the eyes
of the boy behind me
and he fell on the ground,
wailing for Jesus or his
mother as he writhed in pain.
And a young woman tasted
the salt on her tongue
until it grew into a great
bitterness. And some
of the salt blinded a crow
who plunged into a windshield
and died on the hood,
and the driver hit a tree,
his head banging
against the steering wheel,
the horn blasting.
A dog sniffed the salt
and caught me by the heel
with his teeth. I dragged him
for blocks until he whimpered
and fell off, like a bloated tick.
Some of the salt
rose up into the clouds
and then rained over
the grass, parching it.
Men and women sobbed,
their handkerchiefs dissolving
into crystals of salt. White
smoke rose from the pavement.
Wild animals stumbled off
the shoulders of the road
drunk on salt or bad luck.

Man on the Flying Trapeze

He let go of the bar, somersaulting. Below, men held the net taut, and the crowd of eager faces looked up, expecting him to execute a perfect dive into it; instead the man somersaulted through space as if over solid ground. The men with the net ran after him. The crowd followed shouting for the man to come down. The man somersaulted through swarms of bugs and clouds—over green fields until they turned to frozen ground and then to mud. He somersaulted through rain and snow, through smoke and dust storms. He almost hit an eagle, whose angry beak gashed his leg. He broke apart a phalanx of geese. He somersaulted over towns, villages and cities, over rivers and then over oceans and continents. A world away, he kept somersaulting until the air seemed to give way beneath him, and then he fell fast, too fast for his last thoughts, he thought. Closing his eyes, he plunged toward the earth, but before he could crash, the men with the net sprinted across open ground, centering it below him, and he bounced up and down with a big smile on his face as the crowd, out of breath after their long pursuit, clapped softly, worried there might be an encore.

Wet Angel

The angel waded into the river. We didn't expect her to get wet.
We thought she'd slide in like light, untouched by the water,
but it dripped off her when she emerged. She lifted her arms,
her wings damp and heavy on her frail back. Her slender body
was aging but still beautiful. "Love lasts," she said, "Only so
long, like the smell of something sweet floating in the air or a
song that grows quiet in the mind, losing its words and then its
melody, the notes slowly sinking into mud." "Who sent you,"
we asked. "I'm not a messenger," she said, "though I do have a
message." "God sent you," we said. "No," she answered. "But
you're an angel." "Yes, she said, "we live among you." She tried
to fly, running over the soft ground and leaping repeatedly, but
couldn't. Out of breath and tired, she sat on a rock, her head
in her hands, tears running down her cheeks. "I've lost it," she
said. We laughed. She was one of us, only with wings.

Counting Orgasms

My lover counts her orgasms.
It gives her something to do
during sex
besides have orgasms.
She closes her eyes, and the numbers
follow, first evenly, then
in great bursts. Sometimes
I simply blow
gently into her as if
pursing my lips on a velvety reed
and playing a melancholy melody.
And sometimes I use a little chocolate
on my tongue or some Bali Rose
jelly on my fingertips,
rubbing them against her fur,
orchids, long pink ribbons, red grapes.
And my lover cues me
between the numbers,
a little more of this, a little
less of that as if adapting a recipe
from the NYT cooking section.

*

My lover appears in a Nin Andrews poem.
A world beater,
she's the nameless woman
who once counted 27 orgasms.
Nin imagines 27 penises—
penises like tulips or rabbits,
pale pink and soft, but my penis
is no tulip or rabbit;
no pearly handled tool
uncanny in its precision;

it's an intrepid traveler
trekking and camping.
The day my lover counted 27 orgasms,
I counted only 23.
I marked down each orgasm
on a pad of paper—
like flashes of light
on a dark wall or truffles
wrapped neatly in red foil.
When she gave me her tally,
I nodded in agreement and added
four more marks to the page.

*

My lover is counting again
so I lift my head for a moment.
Sometimes I think she's faking
a few or counting
a shiver or a minor shudder
when it really isn't,
but who can map
the boundaries of an orgasm
when each orgasm maps
its own boundaries or charts
its own vital signs, its own
crests and troughs. Sometimes
when she starts counting,
I leave the room
and get a piece of fruit
or look out the window
to see if I can spot a coyote
in the darkness. When I come back,
she's still in ecstasy

or else fighting her way out
of a bad dream, waiting
for me to hold her
and whisper in her ear, it's okay.

Zero

Anything divided by itself
is one, but not zero;
zero is always zero, always
itself. You can count on zero.

Without it you wouldn't know
whether you had a hundred
or a million dollars in the bank.
Of course, the bank may have

reduced your million to a hundred
without your knowing it.
When someone says
there's nothing in it for you,

that could mean zero
or that there's not enough
to make it worth your while,
which is not quite the same as zero.

When they call you a "zero,"
that means they think of you
as a slug or a frog
something with no earning potential.

"Don't be so hard
on yourself," Zero says,
always ready to contribute
to the solution or the problem.

Zeros often make it big
but then they're not zeros;
they're celebrities
or economists.

Everyone wants a paycheck with lots
of zeros before the decimal.
Where would you be
without zero?

Where are you with it?
Zero may not be much,
but there's enough of it
to last you a lifetime.

More or Less

Gurus tell us that "less is more,"
meaning "Don't try too hard
to attain higher consciousness
and it will come."
And when it comes to love
trying too hard always leads
to disaster or someone saying,
"Don't love me so much,"
meaning that your love is exhausting
or perhaps that your lover is
ready to move on, like water
over rocks, to slip past you.
"Poetry should come as naturally
as leaves to the trees," Keats said,
because he knew love didn't come
that easily as he pined for Fanny Brawne
and coughed up blood
on his sweat-soaked sheets. But contemporary
sex experts in the media warn,
"If you don't plan to have sex,
you won't have it," but if you do plan
it, that might cause a problem,
because sex, not poetry,
according to some, should come
"as naturally as leaves to the trees."
But no matter how you add it up,
whatever works works until
it no longer works and then
you can empty the emptiness
from your pockets and meditate
on a world filled with everything
and nothing, more or less.

The Void

Call it the void if you like,
but it's not really void.
Gases float in it, pillars
of cloud. In the void,
particles jostle
and collide like dodgem cars
or women who bonk heads
at the canasta tables.

The void contains a multitude
of voids, each one a universe
of nothing that is something.
There's no emptiness
quite like a bottle
with only a few drops,
or the bed in which now
you lie alone unable to
forget your lover or
erase those days from your memory.

Empty all the air
from your bottle, but it still
won't be empty.
Empty it, but your dreams will
still float and bob
like a bouquet of balloons.
Put your ear
up to a shell, it's a cave
of nothing, but the sea
still calls to you
with its many voices.

If you can isolate the space
between atoms, which is
empty space, if it's space at all,

you can put your finger
on the true void, but really
there's nothing to touch,
though you still might find
a stray atom or even a filament
of hair from another galaxy.

One Hand Clapping

Like a twin, one hand always seeks its brother, but the brother has gone off on his own. Instead of smacking the other's palm, one hand knocks the knots out of the air, bats bugs into high branches. Instead, one hand parts waves of particles, and debris rains down on fallen trunks, dried leaves, and broken bodies. One hand clapping no longer claps, no longer makes a sound that is clapping. One hand clapping is the sound of a storm of blue butterflies, a message blinking red in the distance, a crow's wings falling from flight. One hand claps, but the bully ignores it, and a new kingdom rises from a hole in the ground. And the queen breathes into the ear of her dying lover. A frog croaks. Deer bound over shriveled corpses. One hand returns again and again, fanning the flames of emptiness that blaze through the forest.

Legerdemain

"Enough tricks," she said as her opal earrings disappeared from
her ears, and a parrot flew from her purse, as pink smoke rose
between us. "Enough sleight of hand, enough legerdemain—"
as I pulled an egg from her nostril, a hundred-dollar bill from
her ear, and the bra from under her shirt, as I waved my hands
and said the magic words and watched her float in air, supine.
Against my will, she righted herself and walked through a
door as if only spirit. Before I knew it, she kissed me. "No more
tricks," she said as her black thunderous hair fell loose down
her back, as her jeans split at the seams and fell off, revealing
her turquoise thong. "Okay," she said, "if that's who we are."
Then I was naked, and as the smoke cleared, there was nothing
between us.

Fox at the Door

A fox came to the door, the sun shining on his pretty red coat. "Can you spare a dollar," he asked, his paw extended. "A dollar won't get you anywhere, I said. "It's not worth a cent." I wondered why a fox would want a dollar anyway. The fox shook his head, "Sad times," he said. "Then make it five dollars." I considered that for a moment. I looked at his red fur, which now seemed a little worn, crusted with dirt. "I can't see that five dollars will help you either," I said. "If a dollar's worth nothing, then five times nothing equals nothing. And what's a fox going to do with money anyway?" "I see your point," he said with a smile, but when I went to shut the door, he slipped inside. He sniffed the floors, trotting from room to room. As I followed him, he seemed to ignore me, but I grabbed his tail and then he leapt back to face me. "Okay, I asked, "What'll it take to get you out of here?" "I could ask the same question," he replied. I opened the door and pulled out a twenty-dollar bill, but he laughed and leapt on the bed. "Some things money can't buy," he said and fell into a deep slumber. Soon his smell filled the house, and the snoring was unbearable.

Whistling

In a short dress, the brunette with seven huge jungle parrots
perched on her head, shoulders, and arms sashays under
the palm trees. The wind follows her. The sun touches her
face—her large brown eyes half closed. Arrayed in blue, green,
orange, and bright yellow outfits, the parrots lift their beaks
high as if waiting to snag flies or a small bird that might fly by.
How did I get these parrots? she wonders. How did we get this
brunette? the parrots wonder. The parrots like the thick moist
heat. She doesn't like the oppressive heat, but she likes the
parrots, even though they squabble among themselves at night.
She keeps her shoulders straight and her head up so that the
parrots are balanced, sweat beads welling up her eyes. They
cling to her body without letting their talons bite her skin. As
she walks down the hot pavement, the crowd parts to let her
through. Traffic stops. Men whistle at her. Women whistle at
her. The parrots nod and whistle back.

Bluejays

With angry faces and noisy
slogans, bluejays descend
on trees and garbage,
demonstrating their dissent.

Wires twang in their wake.
The air fills with holes.
They chase phoebes from their nests,
crack open eggs.

They scare finches and chickadees
from feeders full of thistle.
They make treaties with robins,
then break the treaties.

They behead worms.
While downy woodpeckers
pack their scarves in trunks
and book long flights to South America,

while crows squabble in their forums,
bluejays loot stores and shops,
plunder chests of acorns,
planting the seeds of forests.

With crownlike crests
they vanish on gusts of wind—
from thick white clouds,
their blue feathers falling.

Counterpunch

Dancing around the heavy bag, Stevie Ray hunches down, unleashing a flurry of blows and then a knockout punch that dents the gut. The bag gasps and grunts, but doesn't go down. It wobbles from the power of the punch and then steadies itself. "You didn't get me down, Ray," it challenges. Stevie Ray circles his opponent again, focusing on the chest, so he won't be fooled by a head feint. When the time is right, he crouches and then repeats the same combination, a flurry of punches followed by the powerful right to the jaw; only this time, the bag counters with a left to the gut and a powerful right cross. Stevie Ray goes down like a spilled drink. Shaking the cobwebs out, he rises slowly and faces the bag. "The winner by a knockout . . ." "Damn you," Stevie Ray says, "Can't you let me win once?

Adam Out of Paradise

"You should be happy with what
you've got," he says, eating
the red apple in his hand in two bites
and throwing it into the weeds.
He catches a snake by its tail end
and clamps the head shut
before he flings it away.
He sucks the juice out of a plum
even though the birds have shit
on it. "That tastes good," he claims,
"sweet and juicy." His cats
bring him neat packages of money.
His owls guide his every move,
warning him of the pitfalls
and of the bridges not to cross.
His bees bring him so much honey
that his lips are coated with it,
honey smeared on his skin.
And his lover is an ocean.
"You should be happy
for all the small things
life has given you," he says
in his robe of plentitude,
surveying the garden
of beans, potatoes, sweet potatoes
the stalks of corn poking their heads up,
the crows that bring him the news
of their daring flights—
"happy for the small breaths
that issue from your lips, for each one
rises to the heavens and comes back
as rain." Now he bows his head
in gratitude for the spirit
walking in the garden, the flies

he swallows with each gulp of air.
Tears drip from bright webs
and sparks raining from the sky
seed the gashes in the earth.

Ode to Yahweh

I salute your fabulous excursions into pure air,
which, by the way, is not really pure
once you break it down into its elements.
And where have you gone this time?
Are you resting on a cloud? eating
a sandwich with one of your dead heroes?
or perhaps only pissing on the bodies—
forgive the metaphor, because as we all know,
the piss is ours, but you often get pissed,
and frankly, I don't see why you can't piss
since you created it. The dove came back,
its feathers wet and shiny, but no word
from you unless we consider the dove
itself your word. Perhaps you followed
the stream of Monarchs to New Mexico,
and right now you are floating over the Mississippi River.
The onion salutes you, laying down its layers
to lure you back with a delicious pureed soup.
Why have you disappeared so thoroughly?
I shake the bush, no fire or voice.
Snakes leave us in the lurch, parting
the leaves at our feet. The apples
taste sweet and tart but what of good and evil?
Come to think of it, the world is on fire.
So maybe you are all around us,
just quieter and more efficient.
We're bombing the moon. Stick around. We've got
a few tricks that will surprise even you.

How to Walk on Water

It's not difficult.
Just take a deep breath
and forget all those
who have sunk before you.
Forget Jesus, who was genetically
predisposed to moments of flight.
Forget Siegfried
and his winged boots—
that's a trick, an illusion.
Forget anything that might
cloud your mind
or your vision with doubt.
Let your arms lift
as if strings on a puppet.
Keep your eyes open
and focused on the rock
fringed with moss
on the other side.
Imagine your body
as light. Now shine
over the water
and let the waves splash
through you
as the shadows fall
deeper under the surface.
When you get to the other side,
be sure to allow your body
to settle into itself,
to regain its mass.
Now bow your head
and act amazed
as if you've accomplished
a great feat.
Take another deep breath

and open your arms
to your minions.
Thousands of birds
clap their wings

3

Burial

I wish I could say
I put my father in the ground,
that I dug the hole
with the help of my sisters and friends
and lowered him in
and then each of us said some words
and tossed shovelfuls of dirt
and dirt ticked against his casket
until dirt was hitting dirt
and the hole filled.
Then I might now hear him
grumbling in spring—
pushing his stubbled kisser
through the tulips,
asking for a nice big drink
or jabbing the air with his fleshy fists.
Or maybe I'd smell the Wildroot
combed through his black curly hair
oozing from the earth
or I might hear his bones
humming to a congregation
of weeds and tubers
or maybe his legs would kick
toward the sky, sending out
his message, "I'm back,"
and maybe his heart would start
pumping in its cave
and another sales pitch
would roll off his tongue
and he'd rake in the commissions
from all the buds and blossoms.
But no, not a word from "the old man,"
not in this ground, because I delivered
his ashes to the river
and some caught on the rock

and some sunk into the jaws
of catfish trolling the bottom
for lost treasure, and some glued
themselves to the hulls of boats
carrying their cargoes to New Orleans,
and some rode on the wings of eagles
who skimmed the surface of the water
as they flew to their historic homes
on the other side of the river
and some of my father's ashes
sparkled in the muddy water
like seeds ready to burst.

Be a Bigger Person

Be a bigger person, my mother said
by which she meant I should forgive
the pan for hitting me in the head,

the grease for sizzling on my arm,
my sister for stealing my last dollar.
She's right, of course: Everyone

should be a bigger person.
Bigger people wink at each other
when they pass on the street,

like overhead flashing lights,
knowing that they've risen
above their anger.

Bigger people lean against
each other and ripen,
ethylene gas oozing from their pores.

Everyone should let go
of their personal vendettas, grudges,
and the injustices they've suffered

as if tossing carrier pigeons into the air.
Just step back and watch them fly away
with scribbled messages.

Tell yourself the feelings are gone.
Be a bigger person, I say to myself
And now pigeons fly around me

like bats circling the belfry, making
a screechy noise that won't let up
until dawn.

Downpour

In the Hotel Sovereign
my father handed me a bucket
to catch the rain streaming
through cracks in the ceiling.

Then he climbed into a dry
crawl space with his flashlight
and a book. My mother
covered the food

and furniture with plastic
while my sisters burrowed
deeper under their blankets.
Puddles grew over my cuffs.

I splashed through the kitchen
to rescue our pet fly,
his feet stuck to the wall.
The sleepless mice lit candles

and waded through their caves.
Uncle Spider put on
his galoshes tramping
prints all over the walls.

Downstairs in the lobby,
the clerk, sick of calls, took the phone off
the hook and put up a sign
"No Rooms Open,"

and curled up in a hammock.
The buckets overflowed.
The rain never let up.
My mother pulled out her knitting

needle and wove beads
into a curtain, as our
last loaf of bread
drifted toward the moon.

Stories

for Gerald Stern

At the table in his favorite café, he tells me about his lunch
with Ezra Pound, how Pound ate the chopped liver sandwich,
a dollop of it stuck to his lower lip. I listen attentively and lean
in toward the center of the table. Next, he tells me a story about
nailing a famous female poet against a wall and the wild look
in her eye, and the look in his eye is wild. He jumps to his feet,
gesticulating, his voice growing louder. He recites a poem from
his first book. Now he tells me the story of how he tricked the
Nazis into a room and locked the door so they couldn't escape.
Then comes another story about his early days slinging coal,
his face full of dirt, the songs gritty in his mouth. He raises
his arm in air as though lifting a shovel in defiance. "Stop,"
I shout. "No more, please." But he continues with his stories
until he grows dizzy and falls back into his chair while I sip my
tea, remembering my uncle who resembled Trotsky, my sister
whose red shoes had wings, and my former lover, whose legs
were so long she became a tree.

Forgiveness

Forgiveness is a house
with open doors and windows
and voices rushing through,
leaves scattered on the wood floor.

When you forgive,
demons escape from your body.
They ride out on your breath
like bubbles or blinding

rays of light. They sweat
from your brow. They spark
from your fingertips. They walk out
of your bones, wearing your clothes.

When you forgive, the sky grows
denser and darker.
The map of your future
dissolves in your hands.

You bow your head
as though taking communion or receiving
a curse in a graveyard. "Let it go,"
everyone says, but you have let it go

and yet it's still ringing inside you.
Forgiveness comes when you least expect,
like a siren on a crowded street
or the crack before the ceiling gives.

Another Friend Gone

Another friend died
yesterday, in a distant city.
After hearing the news

you watered the houseplants
and tended the purple orchids,
while I walked down to the river

over patches of pitted snow.
Blocks of ice floated
south, bobbing like whales

or toy boats in a bathtub.
Later, crows descended
on the driveway, silent

for a moment, before they
sprang back into flight.
We lit candles

and told stories about him,
though our memory of him
had long ago begun to fade.

Risen

When Dionysius returns, we throw
a sad little party for him.
As always, he rants and raves
about sacrifice and the need for love,
but what has he ever sacrificed
besides others? The gray-haired
nymphs can barely stand,
let alone dance, yet they make a show
of waving their arms in air
and lifting their legs,
their faces red and wrinkled.
Dionysius orders us to kill
a goat, but there is no
goat to kill, so everyone acts
as if the deed has already been
accomplished. In truth, Dionysius
doesn't look so good, his dome
bald, his hair sticking out
over his ears like broken straw.
Someone calls for the cake,
and three nymphs carry it to the table.
I take my bow. I baked
the cake, a frothy buttercream
frosting over thick white
cake with ganache layers.
The head nymph sticks in
one large candle, and Dionysius
lights it, with his famous lighter,
the flame shooting over the cake,
scorching the tablecloth, but the candle
gets lit. He blows it out,
leering at the daughters of the nymphs
who have come to help their mothers
through another ceremony. I cut

the cake and give him the first piece.
He eats his slice in four
bites, frosting dolloped
on his cheeks and chin.
As the music starts,
he steps out on the dance floor
and twirls around, working
himself into a short-lived frenzy
When he collapses, the nymphs circle
around, chanting his name,
believing he will rise again
but he lies on the floor shaking
and trembling. Soon, their daughters
are helping them out to their cars.
The stink rises from his body,
which jerks one last time
and then goes slack. I leave him
where he is and take the cake
back to the kitchen to put
it in a box. When I return,
the place is empty, the lights
are off, and Dionysius has risen.

What They Take, What They Leave

They take the car because you can't
hear the horns blasting
when you drift out of your lane.
They take what's left in your seven
accounts to pay for the special
apartment equipped for old age
and the window with the view
of the five-story garage. They take
the credit cards and shred them.
They take the chef's knife,
scarred and dull, out of your hand,
the bagel toasted until it's rock hard,
the warped bread board
that ripples an inch above the counter.
They take the old couch, the marble
coffee table, the porcelain candy dish
with cracked wings, the Japanese drawings—
said to be worth something.
They leave the steel grips
in places where you have to pull
yourself up. They leave red
buttons attached to cords.
They leave the bugs, crawling
over the tiles, the invisible
torn webs dangling in the corners.
They leave the cracked Royal
Doulton mugs, the 40-year old cigarettes
that crumble to the touch,
the salt-pocked table,
and decades of dust floating
toward the locked windows.

Scattering Our Mother's Ashes in Forest Park

My sister scatters our mother
in the rocks. "She loved the rock
garden and the shade," she says.
I scatter our mother in the pond
under the wooden footbridge.
"Even in this heat, it's cool here."
I watch for a while to be sure
she remains under the footbridge,
but eventually the ashes drift out.
Fourteen years after her death,
we carry our mother's ashes
in a plastic bag and lay her down
throughout the park like seed.
Up the long hill in front
of the museum, past the statue
in the fountain, spouting streams
that arc above shiny coins,
I create a trail of ashes
that leads all the way to the door
of the museum. "Mother wanted us
to love art," I say. I consider leaving
a little bit of her inside the door or under
the Max Beckmann murals, but instead
we remain outside. The sweat beads
roll slowly down my sister's cheeks.
I wipe off my forehead. My clothes
thicken in the heavy humidity.
As if she has received a message
or a text, my sister sets into motion,
guiding us to a sunny spot
of lawn where as a young woman
our mother sunbathed with her girlfriends
and flirted with boys
who pursued her into the park.
"All the boys wanted to date her," she says.

On the lake, lovers row in canoes
or drift, lying in each other's arms.
My sister empties the plastic bag,
and the last pieces of gravel
and bone glisten in the green water.

Patience

"Everything comes to those who are patient,"
my grandfather says, as he blesses his tea,
the steam rising into his face. He believes
that patience is a great shining sea
where small boats head out on the waves
toward a distant shore.
But small boats float and float . . .
and some never arrive.

What if patience is some kind of curse
passed down through a family
like an inheritance that has been plundered
or a worthless family heirloom that you dust
and place on the edge of a crowded shelf,
hoping it will fall and break

And what if the fruit you seek
hangs from a branch and each time
you rise—like Tantalus in Hades—
to eat the fruit, the branch lifts
and each time you dip to drink,
the water recedes from your lips?

"Be patient," my grandfather advises,
"even after your house is empty."
He is long gone, and each dawn,
as the sun rises through the trees,
his windows wait to catch fire.

Old Grievance

The old grievance plunges
through the window of your house,
falling into a daze on the floor.

For a while you watch at a distance,
unsure of whether you should cover
it with a blanket and carry it outside

or take a photo of it. Instead you open
all the windows and doors in your house
and hope that it will fly away.

Because if it dies on the floor,
it will be an omen of worse things to come.
Eager to escape, the old grievance

takes off with its powerful wings,
nearly knocking you down.
You lock the doors and windows,

board up the broken one,
sweep up shards of glass and feathers,
but now another window breaks,

and there's the old grievance on the floor again,
this time sullen and fierce, its beak
ready to rip you apart.

With Age Comes Wisdom

"With age comes wisdom,"
they say, but even
wisdom begins to fail—
like a password whose characters
written in ink
have become blurred,
cloudy figures
in a Chinese watercolor.
Or like a key to a door
that is missing.
When you walk through,
nothing is there but some old
furniture you don't recognize
and a sweater that belongs
to someone else.

The Old Man

The old man should be quiet.
He should let the rotten air
surrounding him dissipate
and drift out the windows.
He should lie still
and let someone love him
or at least not hate him
for a moment.
He shouldn't rail against
the twilight or the waning moon
or the rocks poised to fall on him
or the avalanche an echo
away from burying him.
He shouldn't shout
for his supper or his cane,
shouldn't bellow
as if he were some kind
of forge breathing flames
up through a chimney,
or hallelujah the hell
out of every attempt
to bring him peace.
He should let the light
warm his face and chest
instead of ridiculing your radar,
laughing as you thrash
in yet another sticky net.
He shouldn't choke
the sparrow cupped in his hands
to prove his kindness
and then sip his scalding tea
bowing his head
and whispering
the words of a prayer.
He shouldn't stomp

on mercy while claiming
to be merciful.
He shouldn't tell another story
about a lover he has
hoisted against a wall
or taken mid-air
or turned over underwater
or gored until she
burst into feathers.
Instead he should let
love evaporate
and rise into the clouds.
He should decry only
his own deceit.
He should lie down
and breathe deeply
and wait for the wind
to deliver his final breath
or the dog to prophesy
the instant he will hear
the wrench clink in his heart.
He shouldn't eat the dust
with such relish.
He shouldn't pour his own
ashes over your head.

The Escaped Creatures Offer a Blessing

Bless the flood
that broke the locks
and opened our cages,
that burst through windows
and doors, that broke
down our prisons
into bricks and sticks.
Bless the chaos
that stunned our judges
and jailers and rendered
them helpless.
Small beasts and rodents
fed and sustained us
in the wilderness.
Bless the unstated laws
that ruled our guts,
the codes that spiraled
in our blood and defined
our lusts and cravings,
our animal spirits.
Bless our tongues
that tasted the fire
and the sweetness,
that could foretell
the future written
in the entrails of corpses.
Bless our snouts that smelled
death coming with his nets
and electric barbs,
that allowed us to escape
his traps again and again.
Bless our tails
that learned to lie.
Each time our captors
sacrificed another creature,

the smoke hid us, rising
into the heavens.
And bless our journey,
though it was fraught with uncertainty
and danger, though it led us
from captivity to captivity,
though it was only a moment.

With My Enemy

I spill salt on the table to let him know that this will not be easy and then I brush it off with my forearm. He does the same but leaves a few white crystals between us. We both laugh at our silliness, and there is a kind of warmth in the air that might allow one to mistakenly believe that friendship is once again possible. As if on command, our young waitress appears at the table. His face serious, my enemy orders a latte. "Plenty of foam," he insists. I order tea.

When the order arrives, I blow the steam off, let my lips touch the hot rim of the mug. He spoons the foam into his mouth.

"Why do we still hate each other?" he asks. "All this happened so long ago I can barely remember it."

I nod, but I remember all of it. I imagine a hawk in the rafters above us. And now it's actually there, eyes trained on both of us. "Look up," I say, "into the rafters, our hatred is still very much alive."

"I don't see anything," he answers, then accidentally kicks the table, my tea spilling. The waitress swoops in to wipe away the pool of tea and the salt.

"Small things, we hate each other over small things," he concludes.

The hawk plunges through the window to catch a squirrel in its talons. "Better to hate over small things," I answer, "than nothing at all."

What My Father Heard

Nearly deaf in both ears,
my father heard the clocks
ringing in another deal,
ringing out big bucks who clamored
and clanged like chains
dragged from a car bumper, who bellowed
laughter in their extravagant palaces,
who snapped their fingers
and whistled for service,
and strutted on wingtips. "Give me
that," he said to no one
who could hear him. At home,
he called for room service.
He called his son the names
of bellhops, called his daughters
to change his sheets.
He heard the wind rushing
over the wings of his Buick,
the yammering locusts falling
out of the trees, splatting his windshield.
He heard his hearing aids buzz
for him to listen, but he removed
them and stuffed them in his pocket
so he wouldn't hear his wife repeating,
"Be careful and don't spend a fortune."
He heard his own drunken laughter
with his clients. He heard them say "yes,"
though their lips and bodies said "no."
"If only my damn legs
would work right," he said
as he stumbled toward the car.
He heard the automatic windows
going up and down, the voice
of Dean Martin singing
"Saw a dollar yesterday

But the wind blew it away,
Goin' back to Houston, Houston, Houston . . ."
He saw the sticks crossed,
the crows lined up in trees,
the faces in the clouds,
but he didn't hear the warning
coming through the leaves.
He heard the sky cracking as his foot
pressed the accelerator down.
He heard the rush of speed
and then the sonic boom
of his body crashing the sound barrier,
the crisp crackle of cash
dying in his ears.